Titles in Series S8711

My book of nursery rhymes
My book of animal rhymes
My book of playtime rhymes
My book of bedtime rhymes
My alphabet book
My counting book
My book of colours and shapes
My book of opposites

British Library Cataloguing in Publication Data
Randall, Ronne
    [Opposites]. My book of opposites.
    1. English languages—Synonyms and antonyms—Juvenile literature
    I. [Opposites]   II. Title   III. Smallman, Steve
    428.1   PE1591
    ISBN 0-7214-9570-2

First edition

Published by Ladybird Books Ltd Loughborough Leicestershire UK
Ladybird Books Inc Lewiston Maine 04240 USA

© LADYBIRD BOOKS LTD MCMLXXXVIII

Printed in England

My book of
opposites

by RONNE PELTZMAN RANDALL
illustrated by STEVE SMALLMAN

Ladybird Books

Jumbo is **big**.

Tiny is **little**.

At **night**, Jumbo and Tiny are fast **asleep**.

During the **day**,
they are wide **awake**.

Morning is breakfast time.
Jumbo gets the cereal
from the **top** shelf.

Tiny gets the
bowls from the
bottom shelf.

Tiny puts the bowls **on** the table.

Oh, no! Jumbo has knocked them **off** the table.

After breakfast,
Tiny and Jumbo have work to do.
They hang the washing
on the line **outside**.

When it starts to rain,
they take it **inside**.

Jumbo's clothes go in the **tall** chest of drawers.

Tiny's clothes go in the **short** one.

The rain has stopped!
Tiny and Jumbo are going out
to play.
Tiny's jacket zips up the **front**.

Jumbo's jacket has a belt at the **back**.

Jumbo **pushes** Tiny **up** the hill.

Then Tiny **pulls** Jumbo **down** the hill.

Jumbo has knocked the ball
over the fence.

Tiny crawls **under** the fence
to look for it.

They have lost the ball!
Jumbo searches **up high**.

Tiny hunts **down low**.
Who finds the ball?

Time for some ice cream!
Tiny has a **small** ice cream.

Jumbo has a **large** ice cream.

Jumbo is **big** and Tiny is **little** –

and they are best friends!